mulganai

Thames & Hudson Australia wishes to acknowledge that Aboriginal and Torres Strait Islander people are the first storytellers of this nation and the traditional custodians of the land on which we live and work. We acknowledge their continuing culture and pay respect to Elders past, present and future. We gratefully acknowledge the Kaanju, Kuku Ya'u and Girramay people and Emma Hollingsworth. Thank you for sharing your story.

D1465159

mulganai

A FIRST NATIONS COLOURING BOOK

by Emma Hollingsworth

HELLO,

My name is Emma Hollingsworth. I am a Kaanju, Kuku Ya'u and Girramay woman residing in Meanjin, and I am the artist behind Mulganai. I created this book because there isn't enough Indigenous representation in the colouring world, and I wanted to change that. I also created these colouring pages as a way for people, Indigenous and non-Indigenous alike, to relax and reach a harmonious state of mind, as well as interacting with and learning about my story as a young First Nation woman – and I wanted it to happen in a colourful and creative way.

This colouring book contains stories from my childhood and the present day. Each piece conveys my connection to my culture and beautiful heritage. These stories, told through the stroke of a pen or a dot of a brush, were a labour of love and made for your enjoyment, so light a candle, grab your drink of choice and get your pencils ready.

HEAL COUNTRY

This artwork represents Country and all its inhabitants: animals, plants and humans alike. Here you can see animal tracks, seeds, trees, bushes, waterways and, of course, this beautiful Land we call home.

Our Country is not just the Land; it is all the living beings that inhabit it. It is the waterways and the plants, the seashells and the rocks. It is the soil that holds the echo of our ancestors who once walked these Lands. It is us and we are it.

The Land heals us, provides for us and shelters us. It is time this nation stood together and took care of this Land like my people have been doing for thousands of years. It is time for healing.

SECOND BEACH

I grew up in Second Beach, Queensland, ten minutes from the Aboriginal community of Yarrabah. It was a tropical oasis and every day I woke up to views of the beach, the ocean and, across the bay, the mountains behind Cairns. These views shaped so much of my childhood.

In this piece you can see the palms and the ocean in the foreground, the bay of Cairns in the middle and the mountains at the back. Above the mountains, the vibrant, hot sun is shining. It feels like home.

PALMS IN PARADISE

This artwork celebrates the tropical landscape of Second Beach. It represents the islands, mountains, palm trees and warm sea water that surrounded me as I played on the beach or walked the rocky trails around my home.

RAINFOREST

When the rainforest collides with the beach,
magic happens. As you colour, keep an eye out
for grass trees, ferns, long grass, coconut trees,
palm trees, hibiscus, climbing plants and
Ulysses butterflies.

OCEAN PARADISE

All manner of sea life coexists in the ocean. Various fish, jellyfish, seahorses and many more creatures inhabit the warm, tropical waters. Growing up on the shores of Second Beach, the ocean forms a huge part of my identity. I fondly recall fishing with my family, catching yabbies in the creeks nearby, and helping my dad untangle the fishing nets that would get caught on the oyster rocks.

This artwork is a recollection of those days. The curved lines represent the curve of the shore as it meets the ocean, and within it all the sea creatures exist peacefully together.

CROCODILE

The crocodile is a powerful, resilient creature and its habitat is in the warm waters on the tropical coast. The formless shapes around the crocodile represent the rocks on the shore and the curved lines represent the waves of the ocean.

I created this artwork of a crocodile because it is one of my totems. Growing up we would often see crocodiles swimming about in the ocean and we would always be on the lookout for them while playing on the sand or swimming in the sea.

TURTLE

The turtle is my second totem. It is such a beautiful creature. The concentric circles within the turtle's shell form its unique fingerprint – each one has its own marvellous signature. These circles also represent my connection to the turtle.

Escape to the world of the turtle as you colour the jellyfish, fish and coral that contribute to its habitat, and get swept away by the bold lines in the background representing the ocean's currents.

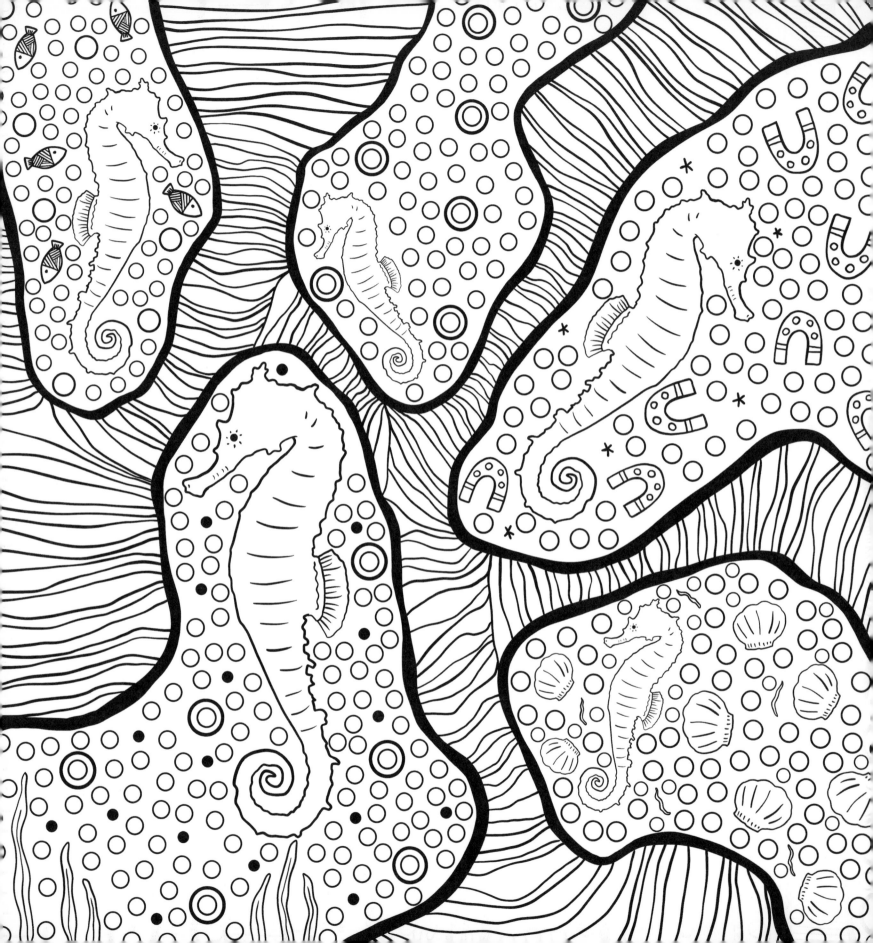

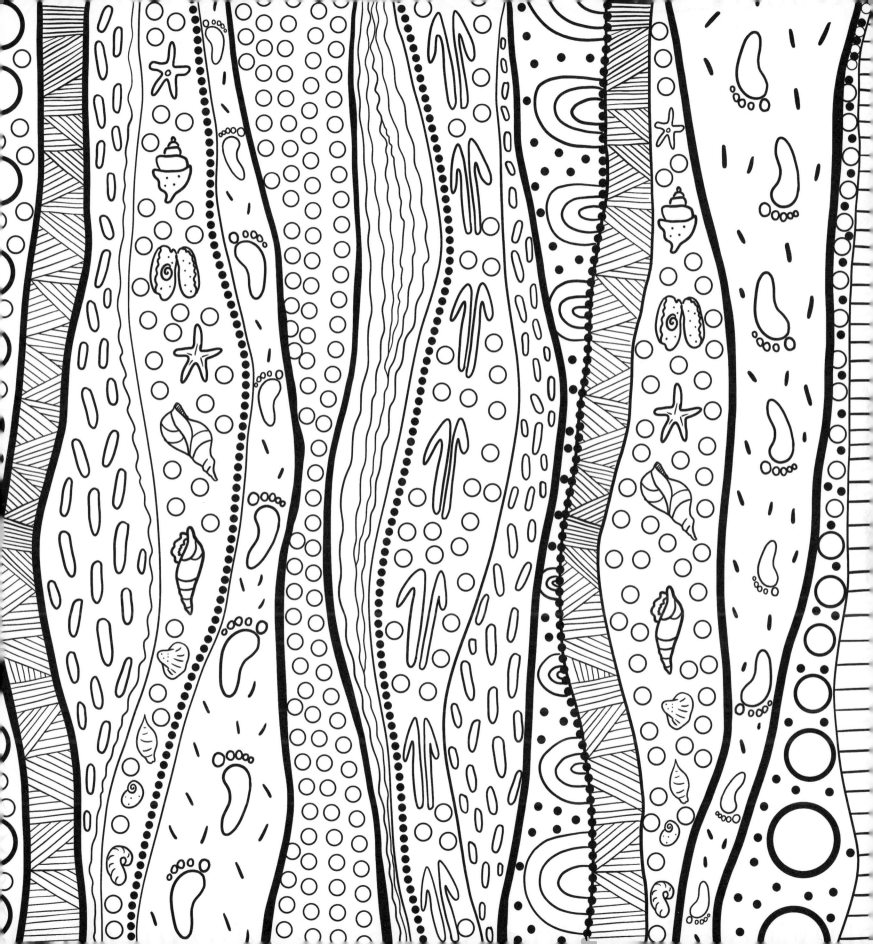

BUDGEBULLA

This artwork depicts the landscape at Budgebulla;
it represents the wildlife, trees, rivers, streams, cattle
and horses that litter the countryside. The road to
Budgebulla is a steep climb through the range. Heavy
rain makes the pass impossible to cross and there
were times when we were forced to turn back. It was
a long, uncertain drive, but it was always worth it.
I always felt very connected to Budgebulla –
it was my second home.

THE CARDWELL RANGE

The Cardwell Range is the only road up to Budgebulla, our traditional Land on Girramay Country. The drive is a beautiful experience, as the landscape can vary from beach, to rainforest, to countryside. There is so much to admire.

JOURNEY TO LOCKHART

Lockhart holds a special place in my heart. We'd visit it frequently when I was a child – always in the dry season, as the wet season brought yearly floods. We'd pass the Iron Ranges and the townships along the way. The landscape was vibrant and green and there were many native animals roaming about. I remember getting bored in the car because the journey took a couple of days. The roads back then were just dirt so it was very bumpy and almost impossible to doze off. But, when we got up onto Country, it felt like we were home.

The journey to Lockhart always had me staring out the window, daydreaming about all the beautiful colours. Choose bright, vivid colours here to represent the happiness these memories bring me.

ROAD FROM LOCKHART TO CARDWELL

The places that meant so much to me as a child, Lockhart and Cardwell, were connected by very long roads. You can see them in this artwork: they're the thick, wavy lines in the centre of the piece. Each of the large circles represents one of the townships that we'd stop at along the way – the places of rest that become so important after hours on the road. In the artwork you'll see two lines with black dots on either side, which represents the coast.

KOOKABURRA

A kookaburra is perched on the branch of a tree.
My family has a connection to kookaburras and
as children we would sit with our cousins and tell
each other stories and superstitions about them.
These peaceful, beautiful creatures are a symbol
of my childhood. I fondly recall watching them for
hours, listening to their songs and dreaming about
the wisdom they could be sharing.

WILLY WAGTAIL

Growing up, my dad would often point out the willy
wagtails and say, 'Look, that's my favourite bird'.
He said they brought him good luck. Nowadays, when
I see them, I can't help but smile and think about what
my dad told me. For him, and now for me, they are
a sign of good luck.

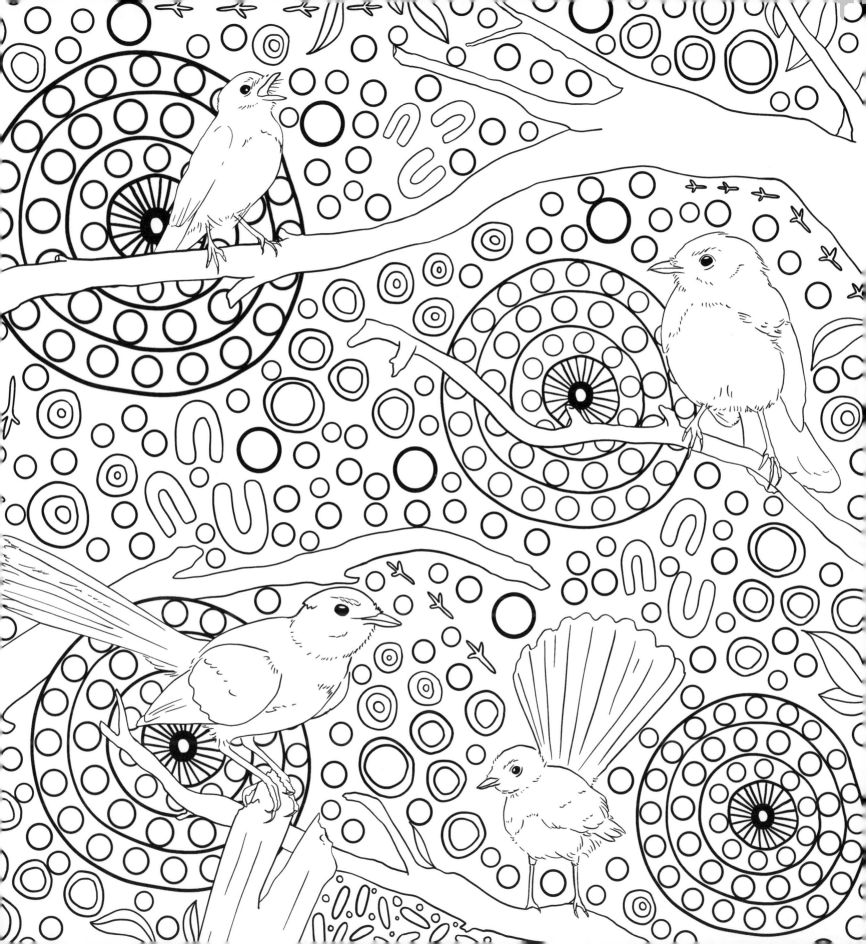

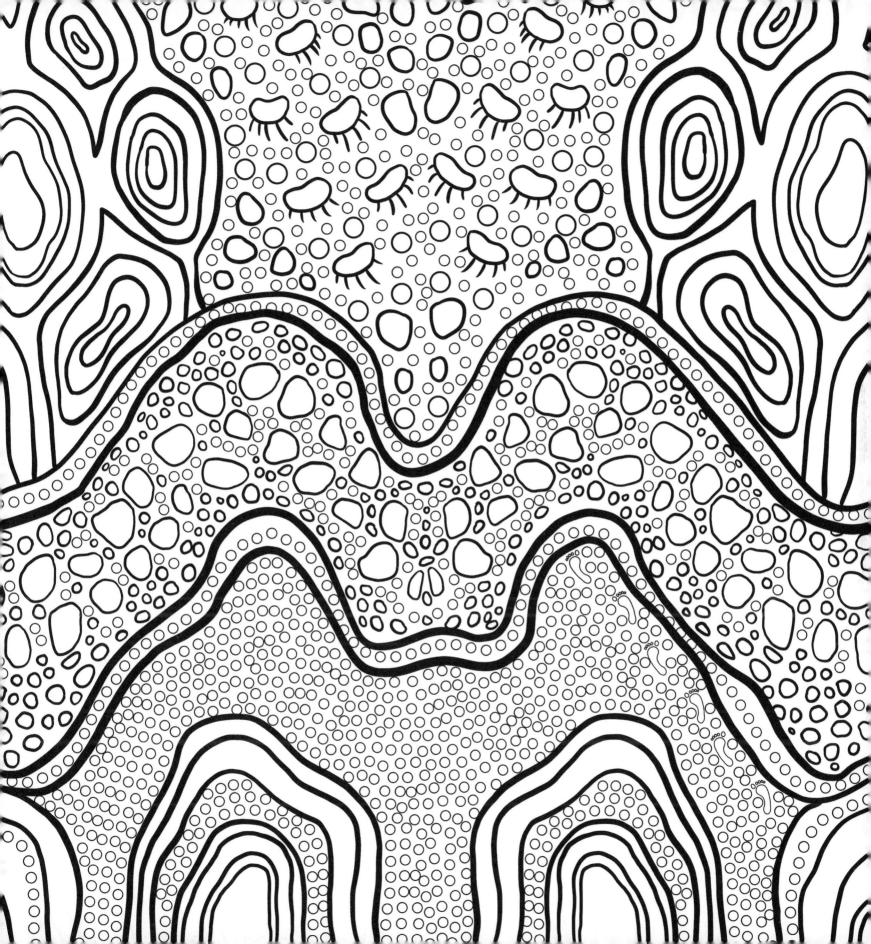

CORROBOREE

The corroboree is a sacred dancing ritual. It is a
very important part of celebration in our culture
and we are taught how to do it from a young age.
The corroboree usually takes place around a fire.
Young people are tasked with building the structure
of the fire by collecting and using old branches.
This artwork represents a celebration amongst mob,
with singing, dancing the corroboree, telling stories
and enjoying *minya* (food).

THE LAND

This piece celebrates the abundance of life the Land gives us every single day. The animals roam free on Country and the Land springs up fresh growth, providing food for the animals and for mob. The creeks flow freely, carving paths through the Land. Fish, crabs and sharks swim in the ocean and mob swim with them, sometimes hunting them for *minya* (food). The mountains stand sentinel, protecting us and the reef from strong cyclonic winds.

PHASES

Artwork appears on the previous page

—

Phases represents hope and courage, the ability to adapt through changing seasons and learning to love oneself. For many, myself included, the last few years have felt like a lifetime of phases. With Covid, the bushfires, the floods and the overall state of the world, the lows hit extra hard. But, so did the highs. Amongst it all, there were personal victories worth celebrating. I came out on top and this painting is a celebration of that.

You'll find my coloured version of *Phases* on the cover of this book. Celebrate your phases, your highs and your lows, by colouring this artwork in a way that reflects you and the phase you're in at this present moment.

DRAGONFLY

I have always viewed dragonflies as beautiful creatures with an almost mythical quality. To this day, I will often sit on the grass, connect with the earth and watch the dragonflies fly by. They are so peaceful and fragile looking, and yet so strong. This artwork celebrates their beauty and the powerful balance between fragility and strength.

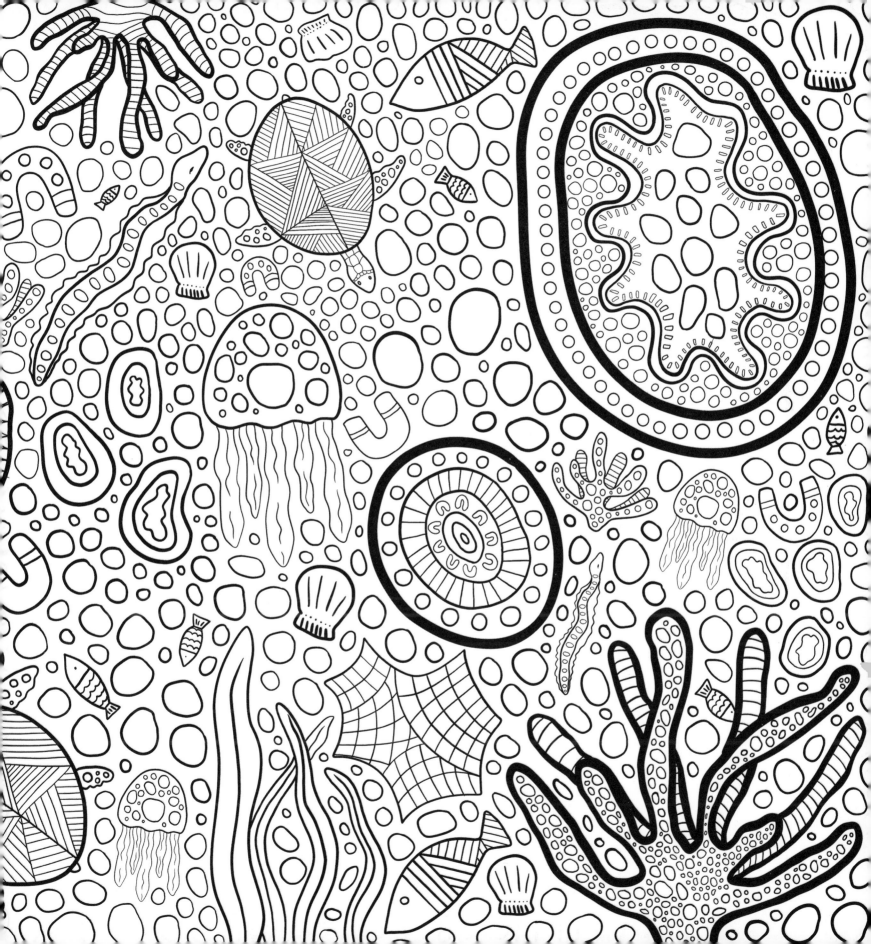

REEF LIFE

Artwork appears on the previous page

—

In 2021, I snorkelled on the Great Barrier Reef, off the coast of Cairns. I was in awe of the sea life within the crystal-clear waters. This artwork is a portrayal of the creatures that live in the reef and the incredible experience I had.

As you bring this reef to life, look out for all its spectacular creatures – turtles, jellyfish, oysters, urchins, fish of all shapes and sizes, and of course, the thriving coral. We all have a part to play in keeping the reef safe.

GECKO

I feel a special connection to the gecko. My first major
artwork was of a gecko that lives in the sandhills on
Country. This colouring page is inspired by that artwork
and a nod to how far I've come on my journey
as an artist.

The large circles represent the communities that are
situated on Country, and the small, irregular shapes
in the background represent the dirt and sand that
the geckos inhabit. Lines connect the large concentric
circles, and these symbolise tracks or roads that
connect these communities.

DINGO UNDER THE SUN

A dingo stands on the Land with the sun beating down on its back. Dingoes have survived on our Land for thousands of years, standing by us mob and serving as loyal hunting dogs.

THREE MOUNTAINS

I am a Kaanju, Kuku Ya'u and Girramay woman and this artwork, *Three Mountains,* signifies my connection to these mobs. Each circle represents one of the three mobs. The mountains are inspired by the mountains that surrounded me in Second Beach and the mountain ranges on Country.

DISCOVERY

This artwork is about discovering your strengths, weaknesses and boundaries, and working on your ability to say no. Self-care is protecting your spirit, your energy and your divine power by putting yourself first and saying, 'I love you' when you look in the mirror and see yourself staring back.

Colouring is one of the most creative forms of self-care. Discover yourself as you colour these pages.

CLEANSE

The paths we take as we cleanse our lives aren't always simple and straightforward. They can be messy, convoluted and at every corner there can be a daunting number of choices and decisions. This painting represents the path I've taken as I've gone through a cleansing phase in my life. Life has been full of many highs and lows and along the way I've felt the spirits of my ancestors guiding me towards growth, personal development, self-discovery and success.

SELF

Artwork appears on the previous page

—

On a journey of connection and discovery, we are all searching for that deeper version of ourselves that lies deep within. This artwork reflects one's inner being.

THE WAY IT WAS

Here, everything we've learnt so far comes together.
This artwork is bursting with symbols – from animal
and human tracks, to meeting places and homes,
minya (food) and tools, and much more. This artwork
represents the balance of life, and it shows how mob
existed in harmony with animals and the Land. There
was a way to things and it was that way for millennia.
We had our rituals, our ceremonies and our technology.
We had our techniques, stories, songlines, systems
and beliefs that we knew and followed to our core.
Our history and our culture is strong and rich,
and as a First Nations woman I will carry that
with me always.

First published in Australia in 2022
by Thames & Hudson Australia Pty Ltd
11 Central Boulevard, Portside Business Park
Port Melbourne, Naarm, Victoria 3207
ABN: 72 004 751 964

thamesandhudson.com.au

Mulganai © Thames & Hudson Australia 2022
Text and illustrations © Emma Hollingsworth 2022

25 24 23 22   5 4 3 2 1

Thames & Hudson Australia wishes to acknowledge that Aboriginal
and Torres Strait Islander people are the first storytellers of this nation
and the traditional custodians of the land on which we live and work.
We acknowledge their continuing culture and pay respect to Elders
past, present and future.

ISBN 978-1-760-76273-5

 A catalogue record for this
book is available from the
National Library of Australia

Every effort has been made to trace accurate ownership of
copyrighted text and visual materials used in this book. Errors
or omissions will be corrected in subsequent editions, provided
notification is sent to the publisher.

Front cover: *Phases,* 2021, Mulganai
Author photo by Michelle Swan

Design: Casey Schuurman

Printed and bound in China by C&C Offset Printing Co., Ltd

FSC® is dedicated to the promotion of responsible forest management
worldwide. This book is made of material from FSC®-certified forests
and other controlled sources.

Acknowledgements

None of this would have been possible
without the help and encouragement of
those around me, so I want to extend
my thanks to all of you. I want to thank
my partner, Justin, for always being my
rock and for encouraging me when I
became a stress head during this project.
I want to thank my family, particularly
my parents, who always believed in me
and supported my dreams from a young
age, and took me travelling around the
country with them. Lastly, I want to thank
Bianca from Thames & Hudson Australia
for guiding me and for being so patient
and encouraging. We worked wonderfully
together on this project, and I couldn't
have done it without you believing in me
and this book.